ALL ABOUT ME!

Art Journal

THIS BOOK BELONGS TO

Walter Foster Jr.

Inspiring | Educating | Creating | Entertaining

Brimming with creative inspiration, how-to projects, and useful information to enrich your everyday life, quarto.com is a favorite destination for those pursuing their interests and passions.

© 2022 Quarto Publishing Group USA Inc.
Illustrations © 2022 Pamela Chen

First published in 2022 by Walter Foster Jr., an imprint of The Quarto Group. 100 Cummings Center, Suite 265D, Beverly, MA 01915, USA.
T (978) 282-9590 **F** (978) 283-2742 **www.quarto.com** • **www.walterfoster.com**

All rights reserved. No part of this book may be reproduced in any form without written permission of the copyright owners. All images in this book have been reproduced with the knowledge and prior consent of the artists concerned, and no responsibility is accepted by producer, publisher, or printer for any infringement of copyright or otherwise, arising from the contents of this publication. Every effort has been made to ensure that credits accurately comply with information supplied. We apologize for any inaccuracies that may have occurred and will resolve inaccurate or missing information in a subsequent reprinting of the book.

Walter Foster Jr. titles are also available at discount for retail, wholesale, promotional, and bulk purchase. For details, contact the Special Sales Manager by email at specialsales@quarto.com or by mail at The Quarto Group, Attn: Special Sales Manager, 100 Cummings Center, Suite 265D, Beverly, MA 01915, USA.

ISBN: 978-1-60058-988-1

Written by Nicole Sipe

Printed in China
10 9 8 7 6 5 4 3 2 1

ALL ABOUT ME!

Art Journal

This is my self portrait

ILLUSTRATED BY PAMELA CHEN & WRITTEN BY NICOLE SIPE

TABLE OF CONTENTS

INTRODUCTION

This art journal is **all about YOU**! It is a time capsule of who you are, at this very moment! In this journal, you will doodle, draw, and write about the things that make you ... YOU. It is your space to record things like:

- what you like
- what you don't like
- what's happening in the world around you
- the important people in your life
- the things you experience every day

And then, one day in the future, you will open this journal again. You will look through the pages, and remember the person you were today. Think of this journal as a keepsake for the Future You!

Are you ready to start creating your time capsule journal? Let's go!

To warm up, start thinking about yourself. Write your name in big bubble letters here, and then write or doodle some things about yourself. How are you unique? What makes you YOU?

TOOLS & MATERIALS

In this book, you will be doodling, drawing, writing, and scribbling. You will also be collecting, pasting, taping, and saving. So, you will need:

- Pens and pencils
- Markers and crayons
- Scissors
- Glue sticks and tape
- Things that you want to save in your book, such as photos, stickers, stamps, lists, notes from friends and family, and news clippings

There is a sticker sheet included with this book, as well as fun things to cut out at the end. Use these stickers and cutouts however you'd like as you decorate your art, journal pages, and time capsule. Use them however you'd like!

Doodle here to test your pencils, pens, markers, and crayons!
Use one or all of your tools as you work your way through this
journal to create your time capsule.

HOW TO USE THIS BOOK

How you use your journal is up to you. You can start at the beginning, or you can turn to a random page and begin there. You can complete your journal all at once, or you can do one prompt at a time over a period of time. The choice is yours! As you complete each prompt, make sure to write the date on the page.

First things first: Write the date that you begin on the opposite page on the "Date started" line.

Last things last: When your journal is complete, come back to page 11 and write down that date too.

Think about when you might like to open your journal again. In five years? Ten years? On your 25th birthday or when you're 99 years old? Choose the year and write it on the "Year to open" line on page 11. When you're done with all of the prompts and ready to put the journal away, write that date on a piece of washi or masking tape. Use that tape to seal the journal so it can't easily be opened. Then put your journal in a safe place. Remember: Do not open your journal until the date you chose! Future You will thank Present You!

Color this page and write down these very important dates.

Date started:

_____

Date completed:

_____

Year to open:

_____

WHO I AM NOW

Here is my name in my best handwriting.

HELLO
my name is

_ _ _ _ _ _ _ _ _ _ _ _

Here is my name when I write with my other hand.

HELLO
my name is

_ _ _ _ _ _ _ _ _ _ _ _

DATE: _____

This is my age drawn in big bubble letters.

This is how many candles will be on my next birthday cake.

DATE: _____ 13

THIS IS HOW TALL I AM.

Find a long piece of string. Ask someone to cut the string to your height. Use the string to create a shape on this page and paste it down. How tall are you in inches or centimeters?

DATE: _____

THIS IS MY HAIRSTYLE.

DATE: _____

THIS IS AN OUTLINE OF MY HAND.

DATE: _____

THIS IS AN OUTLINE OF MY FOOT.

DATE: _____

This is a map showing where I was born,
where I live now, and where I go to school.

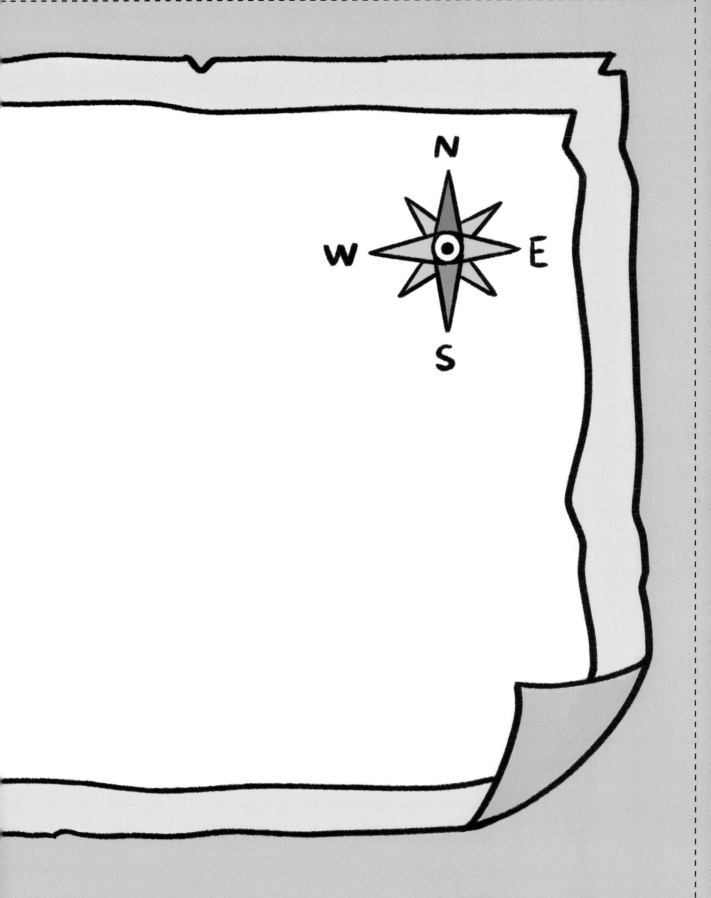

MORE ABOUT ME!

This is something that's interesting or unique about me.

_____

_____

This is what I am most excited about right now.

_____

_____

This subject in school is easiest for me.

_____

_____

This is the most important thing to me.

_____

_____

These are the most important people in my life.

_____

_____

This is one of my
many talents.

_____

_____

This is my favorite thing
about myself.

_____

_____

This always makes me laugh.

_____

_____

This is something that
scares me.

_____

_____

This is something I've done
that I'm proud of.

_____

_____

DATE: _____

THIS ONE OF MY HAPPIEST MEMORIES.

Describe your memory here.

THESE ARE DRAWINGS OF THE THINGS THAT MAKE ME HAPPY.

WHAT I AM DOING NOW

There is always something to draw, no matter where you are. Just open your eyes and look! Let's pretend to take a photo of what's around you right now.

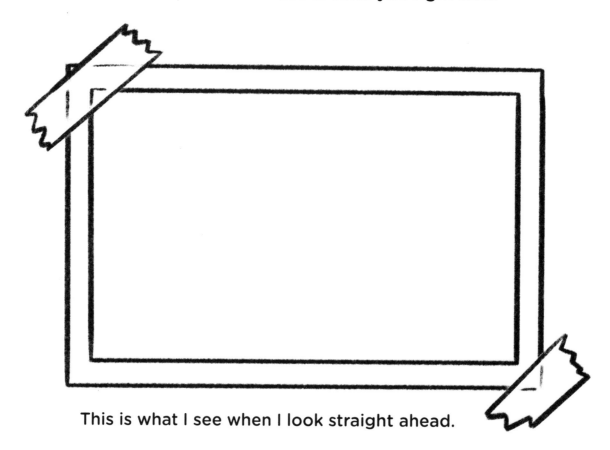

This is what I see when I look straight ahead.

1. Stand in one place. Make a circle with your thumb and forefinger, using your non-dominant hand.

2. Close one eye.

3. Hold your circled fingers an inch away from your open eye.

4. Grab your pen with your other hand and get ready to draw.

5. Start by looking straight ahead. Draw ONLY what you see through the circle. Remember: You're acting like a camera! You're only drawing a small part of the scene.

6. Now repeat and look to the left and right.

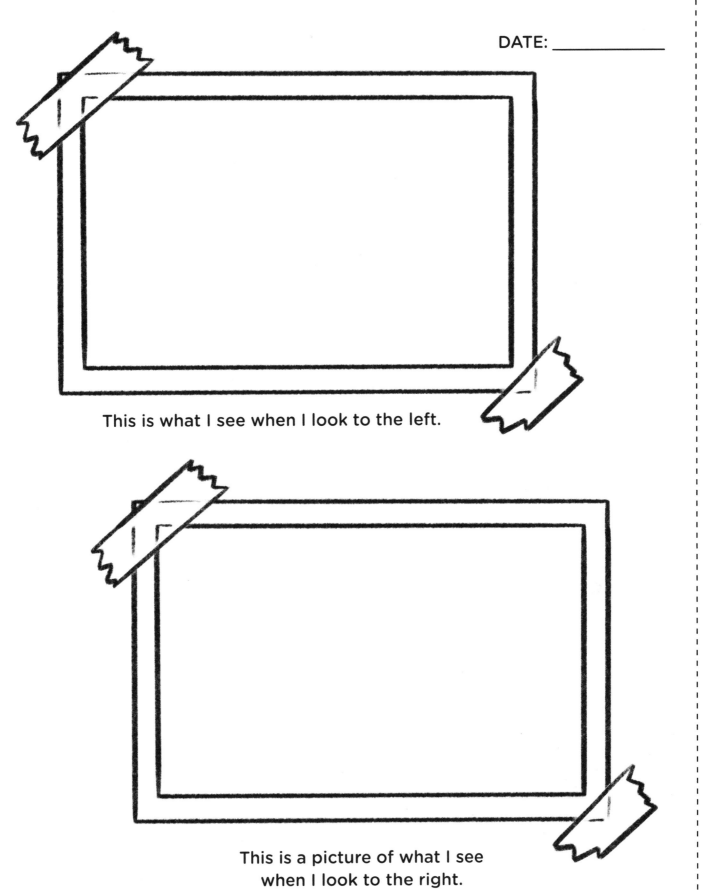

DATE: _____

This is what I see when I look to the left.

This is a picture of what I see
when I look to the right.

WHEN I CLOSE MY EYES, THIS IS WHAT I HEAR.

Fill in the details so this looks like you!

WHEN I CLOSE MY EYES, THIS IS WHAT I SMELL.

DATE: _____

THESE ARE THINGS I LIKE TO WEAR.

THESE ARE THINGS I LIKE TO EAT AND DRINK.

BREAKFAST

LUNCH

Draw here!

DINNER

_____

_____

_____

_____

_____

_____

SNACKS

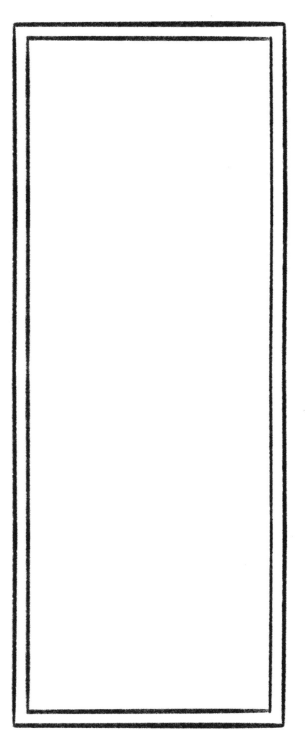

This is the time I wake up.

This is the time I go to sleep.

Last night, I dreamed about...

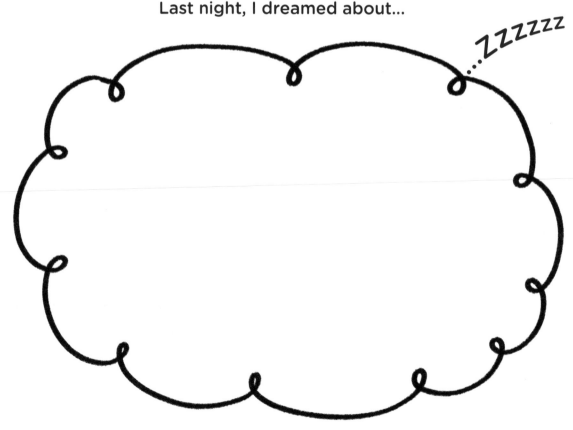

ZZZZZZ

DATE: _____

This is what I do during the week.

WEEKLY PLAN

Monday _____

_____

Tuesday _____

_____

Wednesday _____

_____

Thursday _____

_____

Friday _____

_____

Saturday _____

_____

Sunday _____

_____

THESE ARE THE LAST FIVE BOOKS I READ.

Write the titles on these books!

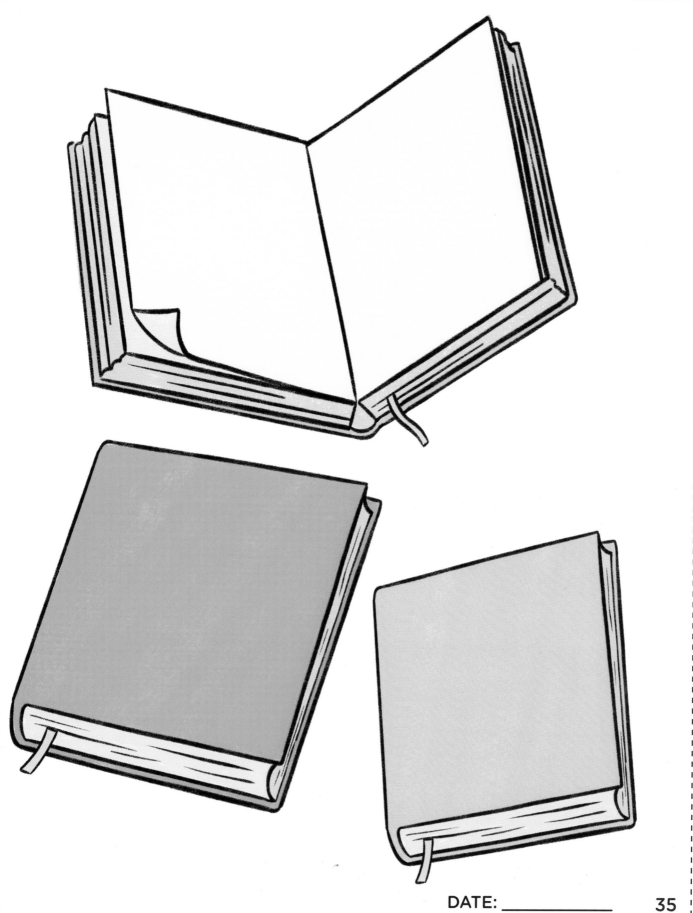

DATE: _____ 35

IF I COULD...

Answer all the questions below, and choose one to draw.

This is something I want to learn how to do.

_____

If I had the house to myself for the day, this is what I would do.

_____

If I could buy whatever I wanted from the store, this is what I would get.

_____

If I could have any pet, this is what it would be.

_____

If I could change anything in the world, this is what I would change.

_____

DATE: _____

Write or draw your answers!

TODAY'S PLAN

If I could spend the day however
I wanted, this is what I'd do.

DATE: _____

IF I COULD BE AN ANIMAL, THIS IS WHAT I'D BE.

DATE: _____

If I were a superhero, this would be my superpower.
Here I am showing off my power!

DATE: _____

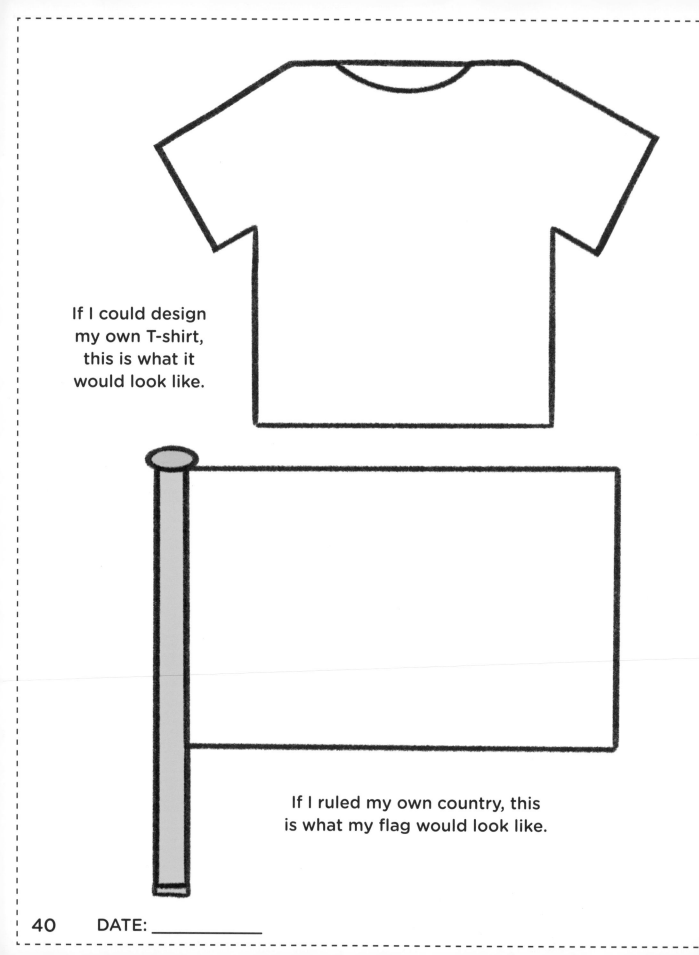

If I could design my own T-shirt, this is what it would look like.

If I ruled my own country, this is what my flag would look like.

40   DATE: _____

If I started my own business, this is what I would do.

If my life were a movie, this is what the movie poster would look like.

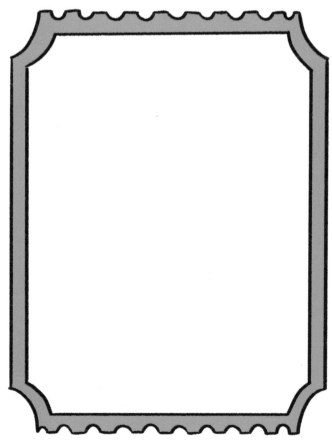

DATE: _____

IF I COULD HAVE THREE WISHES GRANTED, THIS IS WHAT THEY WOULD BE.

1:

2:

3:

DATE: _____

If I could design my own fort or treehouse,
this is what it would look like.

~~~~~~

If I could create my own playground,
this is what I would have in it.

IF I COULD BUILD A HOUSE, THIS IS WHAT IT WOULD LOOK LIKE.

Make sure to describe all the cool features!

| Slides instead of stairs? | A wall made of candy dispensers? | A swimming pool in the bathroom? |

DATE: _____

IF I COULD PLANT MY OWN GARDEN, THIS IS WHAT I WOULD GROW.

DATE: _____

MY HOME

Doodle or write anything that comes to
mind when you think, "This is my home..."

DATE: _____

These are the things my family and I like to do together at home.

1:

2:

3:

DATE: _____

This is a map of my neighborhood.

DATE: _____

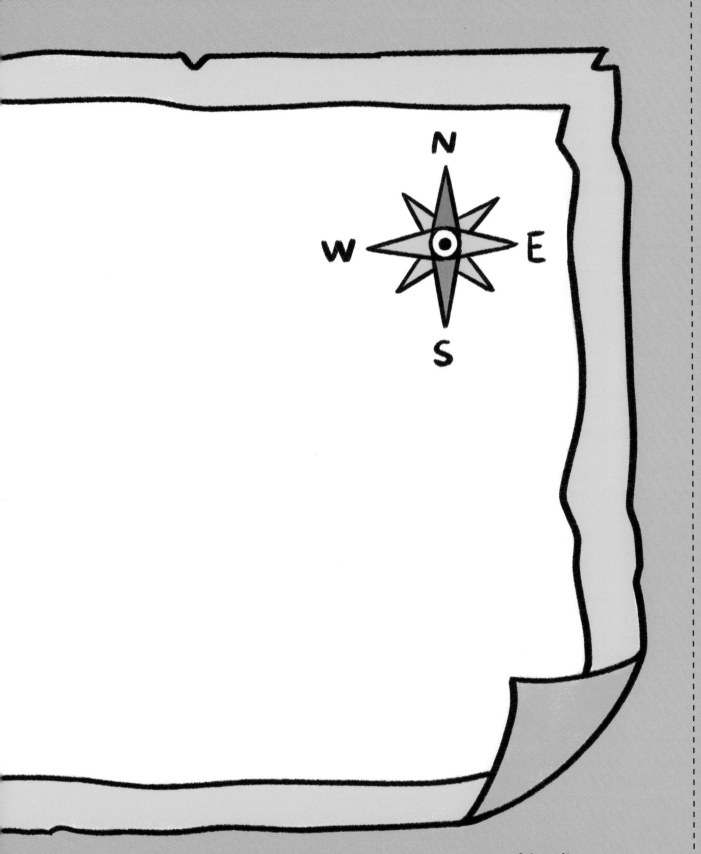

Make sure to label important spots, like the bus stop, your friend's house, or the best places to ride your bike or play basketball.

When I look out my front door, this is what I see.
(Are there any people? What are they doing?)

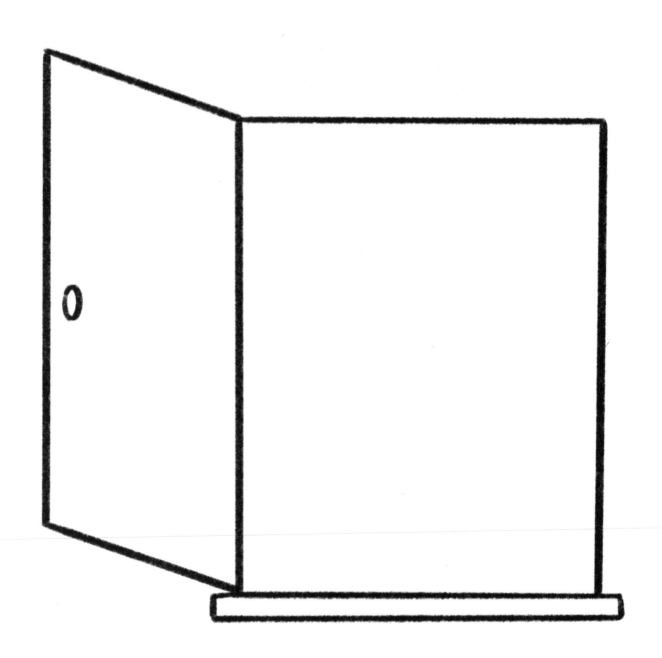

DATE: _____

Now that you're outside, close your eyes.
Write down everything you hear.

Make this look
like you!

DATE: _____

HOW DOES YOUR GARDEN GROW?

Collect any leaves, flowers, bark, or foliage that catch your eye. Rub some dirt onto the page, if you feel like it! Tape or paste your nature collection onto these pages.

DATE: _____

Find something interesting that's on display in your house, like a photo of someone you don't recognize, a painting, or knickknack on a shelf. Ask someone in your family who knows its history. Draw it here and write the story on the next page.

DATE: _____

IN MY HOME...

These are the sounds
I hear at home.

_____

_____

This is what my home
smells like.

_____

_____

This is my favorite room
in my home.

_____

_____

This is something in my home
that ends with the letter S.

_____

_____

This is something in my home
that starts with the letter S.

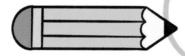

_____

_____

This is the yummiest thing
I like to eat at home.

_____

_____

These are the words
I use to describe my home.

_____

_____

These are the chores I help
with around the house.

_____

_____

This is what I like to do
when I'm at home.

_____

_____

This is how many rooms
there are in my home.

_____

_____

DATE: _____

This is what my bedroom looks like from above.

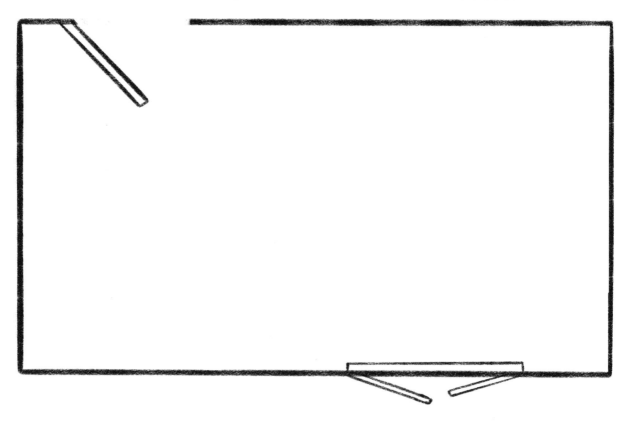

When I look out my bedroom window, this is what I see.

DATE: _____

DOODLE SOME OF YOUR ANSWERS IN THE OPEN SPACES!

This is all the stuff on my bedroom floor (other than furniture).

These are the things on my bed right now.

This is my favorite thing in my room.

This is my least favorite thing in my room.

These are the things under my bed right now.

This is what is hanging on my bedroom walls.

DATE: _____ 59

MY FAMILY

These are all the people and animals who live in my house.

Draw your family and pets peeking out of the windows and door.

60   DATE: _____

This is a portrait of a special member of my family.

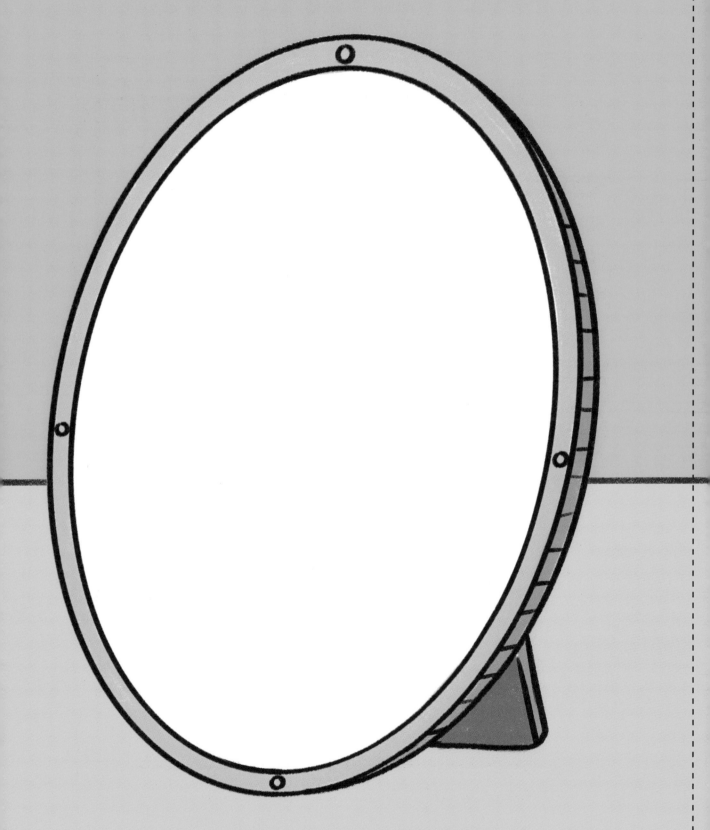

This is one of our family traditions. (Can't remember a tradition?
Ask an older family member to remind you of some.)

FAMILY TRADITIONS

DATE: _____

This is the family member that I look like the most.

This is the family member that I act like the most.

Every family is unique, just like every tree! Cut out the apple shapes at the end of this book (page 119) to fill out your family tree.

MY FAMILY TREE

DATE: _____

Write each family member's name on an apple, and then place them all somewhere on your tree. Keep going until your family tree is complete.

Don't forget to include yourself!

THIS IS ONE OF MY FAVORITE FAMILY DINNERS.

Think about your favorite family dinner. Ask your parent for the recipe and write it down here. Then, draw what the prepared dish looks like, or paste a photo of the dish onto the next page.

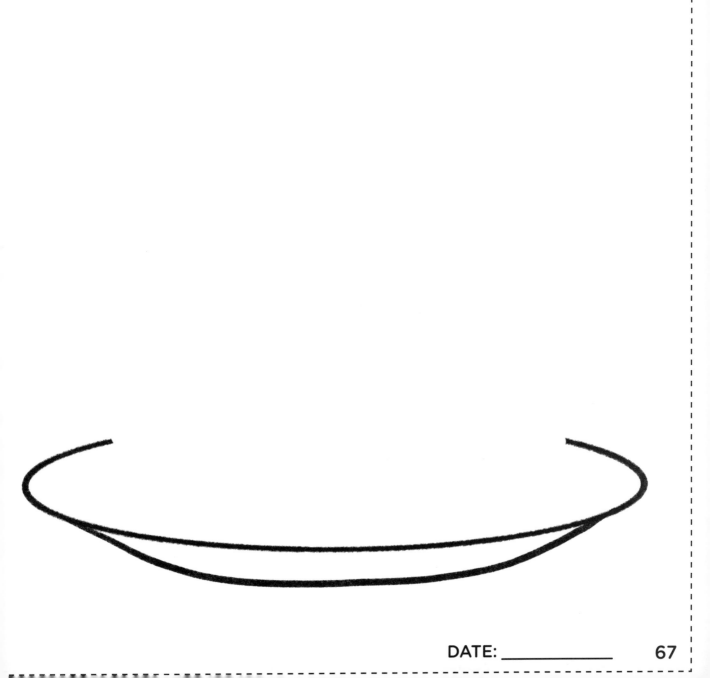

FAMILY QUESTIONS

Ask everyone in your household to write the answers to these questions on a piece of paper. Read the questions out loud to each person and give them some time to write their answers. Have them fold up their piece of paper and tape it on the next page. It's OK to take a peek at their answers!

1. What do you call me?

2. What are three words that describe me?

3. What is something that I always say?

4. What is your favorite thing about me?

5. What do you like to do with me?

6. What is your favorite memory of me?

7. What is something that we both have in common?

8. What am I really good at?

9. Which character in a book, movie, or TV show do I remind you of?

10. What do you look forward to doing with me?

DATE: _____

TAPE EVERYONE'S ANSWERS HERE!

If another family wants to hear your answers, get more sheets of paper and do it for them too! They can keep the answers or let you tape them here.

OTHER PLACES

This is what the outside of my school looks like.

This is what my classroom looks like.

DATE: _____

This is my favorite place to go on weekends.

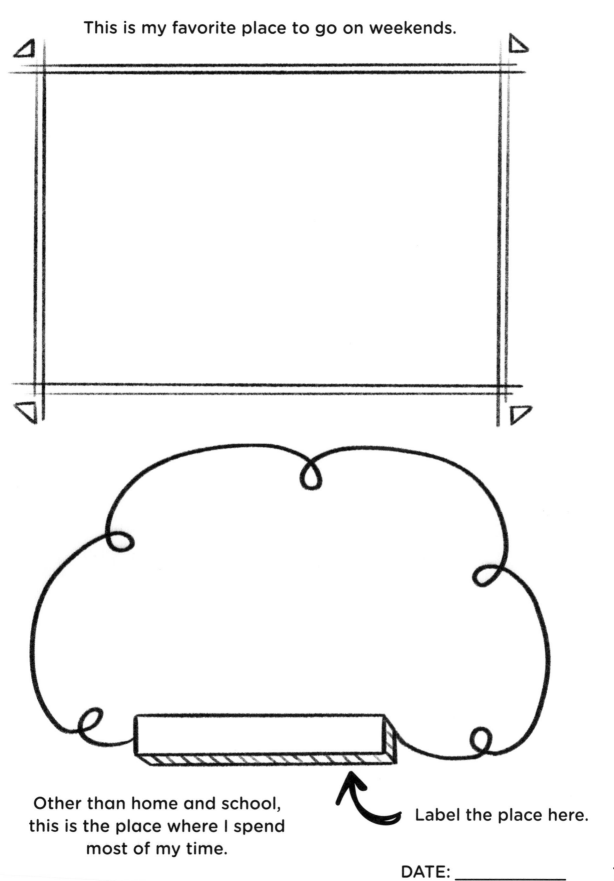

Other than home and school, this is the place where I spend most of my time.

Label the place here.

WINTER

THESE ARE THE PLACES
I LIKE TO VISIT DURING
THE YEAR.

SPRING

DATE: _____

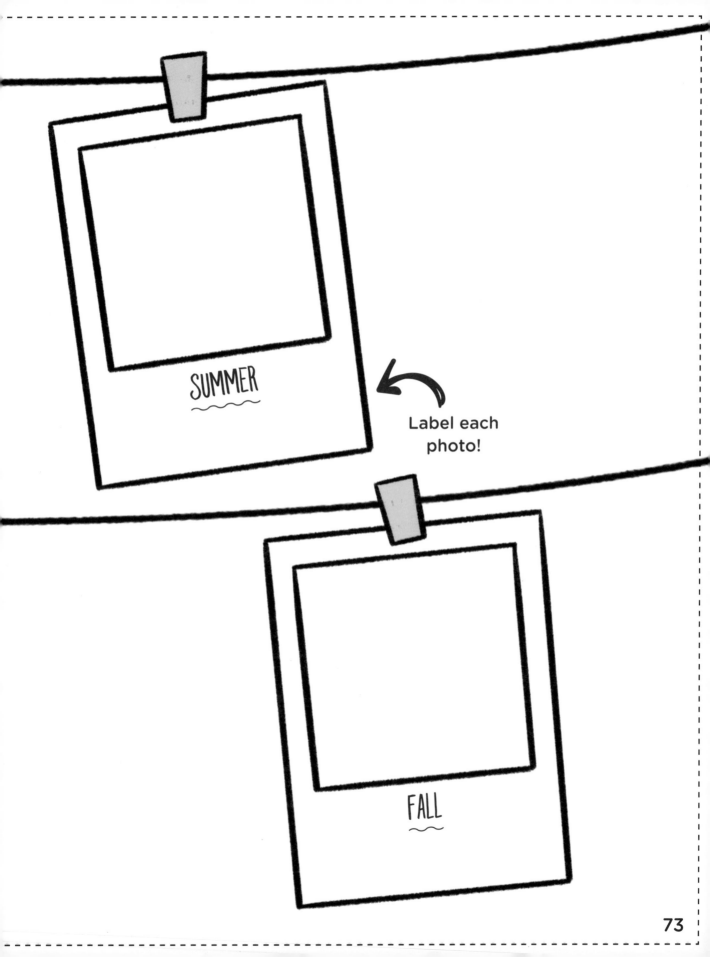

SUMMER

Label each photo!

FALL

This is the best place that I went to this year.

_____

This is what I most remember from my last trip.

_____

This is a famous landmark that I want to visit.

_____

These are the three countries I most want to visit.

_____

This is the planet I wish I could visit.

_____

I HAVE TRAVELED BY:

DATE: _____

☐ Car
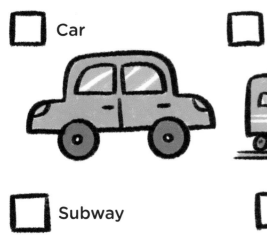

☐ Train

☐ Bus

☐ Subway

☐ Horse

☐ Scooter

☐ Truck

☐ Airplane

☐ Helicopter

☐ Motor home

☐ Tandem bicycle

☐ Hot-air balloon

These are the things I like to take with me on a trip.

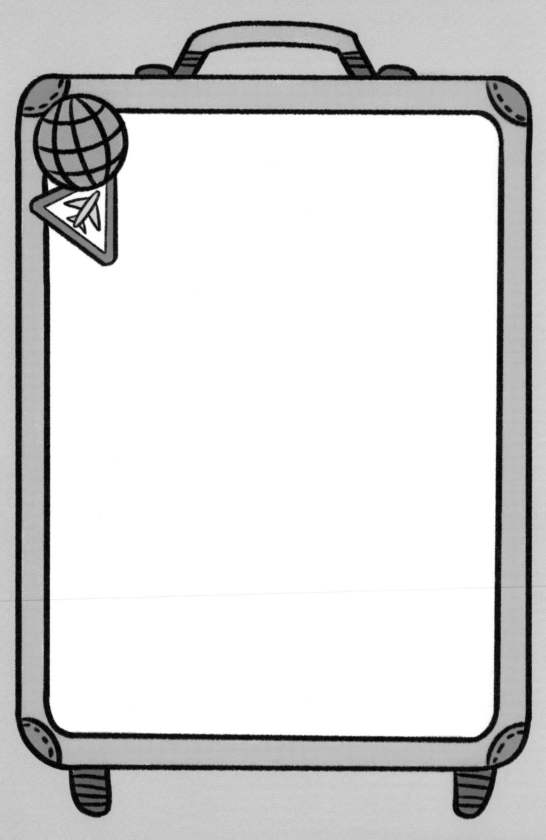

DATE: _____

This is where I want to go on vacation.

DATE: _____

WHAT DO YOU SPY WITH YOUR LITTLE EYE?

The next time you go somewhere special,
complete this page by drawing what you see!
Can you draw something for each letter?

Make sure to write
down what you saw in
this space!

T

R

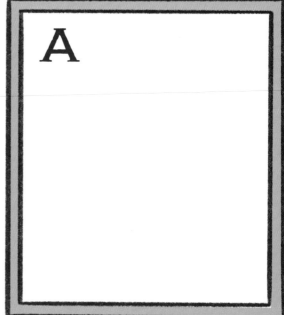

A

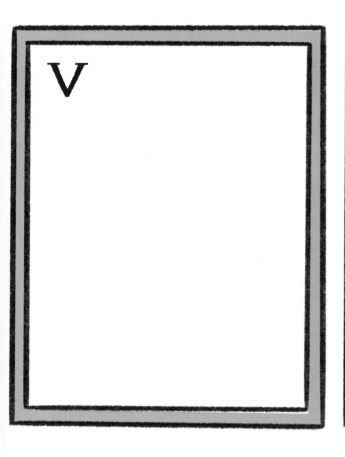

PEOPLE I KNOW

Pretend this is a yearbook page. Ask people you know to sign this book and write you a little note!

AT MY AGE...

Find an older family member or family friend to interview.
Have them help you fill out these facts! Ask your family member
to show you a photo of themselves when they were your age.
Take a photo today too, and paste both pictures below.

Here are some facts about _____.
                                          (name)

at my age   today

DATE: _____

_____ was born in _____
(name)   (year)

to _____ and _____.
   (mother's name)   (father's name)

_____ had _____ children, and now has
(name)   (number)

_____ grandchildren. When young, _____
(number)   (name)

went to _____ and worked as a(n)
        (school name here)

_____. Now _____ loves to
(job)   (name)

_____. Together, _____ and
(something they're   (name)
passionate about)

I like to _____. When I'm the same age as
          (thing to do)

_____, I'll be _____ in the year
(name)   (age)

_____.
(date)

LET'S PLAY A GAME TO SEE WHO KNOWS WHOM BETTER!

Read the questions out loud with a friend. Each of you write your answers on a separate piece of paper. When you're done, read the questions out loud and compare your answers. How well do you know each other?

Paste your friend's photo here, or ask them to draw a self-portrait!

1. Which of these appetizers would your friend order at a restaurant?
a. Mozzarella sticks
b. Onion rings
c. Chips and guacamole or salsa
d. Chicken wings or strips

2. Where would your friend like to go on vacation?
a. To a big city
b. To a National Park
c. On a cruise
d. To visit family

3. What would your friend rather watch?
a. A TV show
b. A concert
c. A movie
d. A YouTube video

4. What kind of game would your friend rather play?
a. A card game
b. A board game
c. A video game
d. A sports game

5. What pet would your friend rather have?
a. A cat or dog
b. A hamster or rabbit
c. A horse or pony
d. A fish or reptile

6. Which chore would your friend choose?
a. Doing the dishes
b. Vacuuming
c. Washing and folding laundry
d. Raking leaves

7. Which of the following does your friend like the most?
a. Reading
b. Watching TV and movies
c. Playing games
d. Playing outside

8. If they could choose, your friend would rather...
a. Go to the movies
b. See a play or musical
c. Watch a dance show
d. Attend a music concert

9. If your friend could be an animal, which would they choose?
a. An adorable little animal, like a chipmunk
b. A super smart animal, like an elephant
c. An animal that can fly, like a bird
d. A big, strong animal, like a lion

10. If your friend had a billion dollars, they would...
a. Buy lots of fun things
b. Buy stuff for friends and family
c. Donate it to a good cause
d. Save it for the future

ANSWER KEY

1-3 answers correct – Maybe you're new friends, or maybe your friend is unpredictable! Either way, that means there's a lot of fun to come.

4-6 answers correct – You know your friend pretty well, but there are definitely more interesting things to learn!

7-9 answers correct – Even the best of friends learn new things about each other every day!

10 answers correct – You know everything about your friend! Can you read their mind?

How many answers did you get correct? You:_____ Your friend:_____

What did you learn about your friend? (Your answer) _____

_____

What did you learn about your friend? (Your friend's answer) _____

_____

_____

DATE: _____   85

AT THE DOCTOR...

Answer these questions the doctor might ask you during a visit.

My doctor's name is_____

When was your last visit to the doctor? _____

How do you feel today? _____

Have you ever had surgery?

_____

Do you have any allergies?

_____

What junk foods do you eat?

_____

_____

_____

What medicines or vitamins do you take?

_____

_____

What healthy foods do you like to eat?

_____

_____

_____

Have you ever broken a bone? If so, which bone(s)?

_____

_____

What do you do for exercise?

_____

_____

My dentist's name is_____

This is how many

teeth I've lost_____

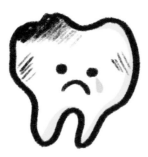

This is how many

cavities I've had_____

This is what I imagine the
Tooth Fairy looks like:

This is my favorite flavor of

toothpaste_____

These are all of my teachers this year and the subjects they teach.

_____

_____

_____

_____

_____

_____

**This teacher assigns
the most homework:**

_____

This teacher is the funniest:

_____

This teacher is the most interesting:

_____

I learn the most in this teacher's class:

_____

DATE: _____

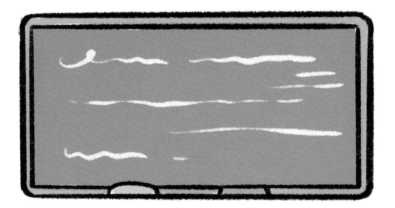

DATE: _____

This teacher's classroom is
the most decorated:

_____

_____ is my favorite teacher, and this is why...

_____

_____

_____

_____

Draw something that reminds you
of your favorite teacher.

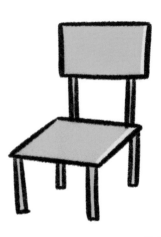

MY FAVORITES

List all of your favorites below.

○ These are my favorite subjects in school.

○ This is my favorite hobby.

○ This is my favorite color.

○ This is my favorite movie.

○ This is my favorite famous person.

DATE: _____

- ○ This is my favorite restaurant.

- ○ This is my favorite TV or YouTube show.

- ○ This is my favorite time of day.

- ○ This is my favorite park.

- ○ This is my favorite place to play.

DATE: _____

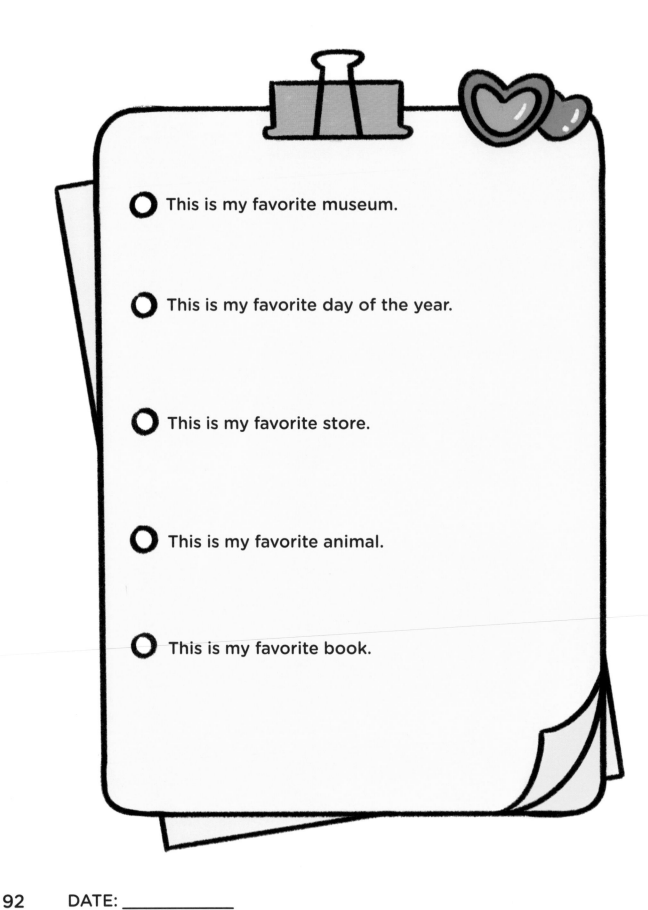

○ This is my favorite museum.

○ This is my favorite day of the year.

○ This is my favorite store.

○ This is my favorite animal.

○ This is my favorite book.

DATE: _____

Listen to your favorite song with your eyes closed.
Draw on this page while listening to the song.
Don't worry about creating a masterpiece.

Just let your marker or
pencil feel the beat.

Lines, squiggles, and
dots are all good!

Make sure to write down the name
of the song you're listening to.

This is my favorite outdoor activity.

This is my favorite indoor activity.

94   DATE: _____

This is a memory of my favorite birthday.

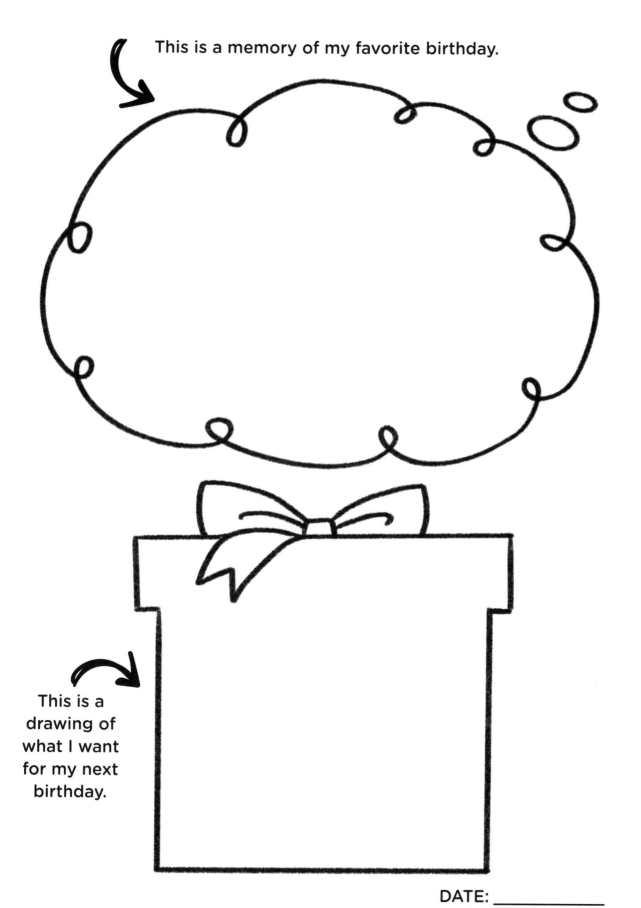

This is a drawing of what I want for my next birthday.

DATE: _____ 95

Color the stars to rate how you feel about:

Rainy days ☆ ☆ ☆ ☆ ☆

Salad ☆ ☆ ☆ ☆ ☆

Haircuts ☆ ☆ ☆ ☆ ☆

Video games ☆ ☆ ☆ ☆ ☆

School ☆ ☆ ☆ ☆ ☆

Bananas ☆ ☆ ☆ ☆ ☆

Surprise parties ☆ ☆ ☆ ☆ ☆

Baking ☆ ☆ ☆ ☆ ☆

Football ☆ ☆ ☆ ☆ ☆

Television ☆ ☆ ☆ ☆ ☆

Cats ☆ ☆ ☆ ☆ ☆

Waking up early ☆ ☆ ☆ ☆ ☆

Swimming ☆ ☆ ☆ ☆ ☆

Chores ☆ ☆ ☆ ☆ ☆

Tennis ☆ ☆ ☆ ☆ ☆

Puzzles ☆ ☆ ☆ ☆ ☆

Skateboarding ☆ ☆ ☆ ☆ ☆

Reading ☆ ☆ ☆ ☆ ☆

Ice cream ☆ ☆ ☆ ☆ ☆

Roller skating ☆ ☆ ☆ ☆ ☆

Dogs ☆ ☆ ☆ ☆ ☆

DATE: _____ 97

Now come up with some things to rate, draw them, and fill in the stars to show how much you like them. Use some of the colorful star stickers for your ratings or color them in!

_____ ☆ ☆ ☆ ☆ ☆

_____ ☆ ☆ ☆ ☆ ☆

_____ ☆ ☆ ☆ ☆ ☆

_____ ☆ ☆ ☆ ☆ ☆

_____ ☆ ☆ ☆ ☆ ☆

_____ ☆ ☆ ☆ ☆ ☆

_____ ☆ ☆ ☆ ☆ ☆

_____ ☆ ☆ ☆ ☆ ☆

_____ ☆ ☆ ☆ ☆ ☆

_____ ☆ ☆ ☆ ☆ ☆

_____

_____

_____

_____

_____

_____

_____

_____

_____

_____

This is my favorite holiday: _____

This is my favorite season: _____

This is my favorite type of weather: _____

This is my favorite outfit: _____

This is my favorite game: _____

This is my favorite pet: _____

This is my favorite sport: _____

This is my favorite emoji: _____

This is my favorite color: _____

This is my favorite superhero: _____

This is my favorite toy: _____

This is my favorite song: _____

This is my favorite word to say: _____

This is my favorite sound: _____

This is my favorite smell: _____

This is my favorite thing to do on a rainy day: _____

This is my favorite thing to do on a sunny day: _____

MY FAVORITE FOODS

Birthday cake flavor: _____

Sandwich: _____

Breakfast food: _____

Dessert: _____

Fruit: _____

Vegetable: _____

Crunchy snack: _____

Soft snack: _____

This is my favorite activity in gym class: _____

This is my least favorite activity in gym class: _____

YOU ARE WHAT YOU EAT!

Collect the wrappers from some of your favorite foods. Make sure they are clean and dry. Then tape or paste them on this page. You can also collect the stickers from fruit, sticks from ice pops, candy wrappers, gum wrappers, or receipts from restaurants you visited with your family.

THE FUTURE ME

Write the rest of the current year in big bubble letters. Decorate inside the letters with things that have happened this year.

Now think about what year you want to open this book.
10 years from now? 20 years from now? Longer than that?
Draw the rest of that year in big bubble letters and decorate
it with what you want to happen in that year.

Write a letter to your future self. Stick the paper in an envelope, and then paste the envelope to this page. Decorate the envelope, and address it to your future self. Don't forget to draw a stamp on the upper right corner!

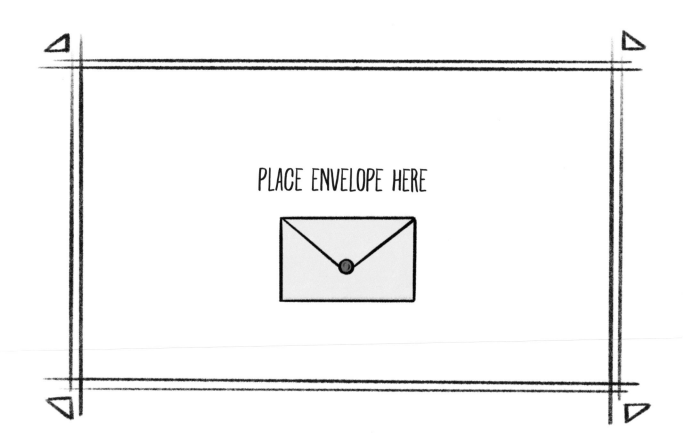

PLACE ENVELOPE HERE

Find a coin from this year. Find another coin from the year you were born.

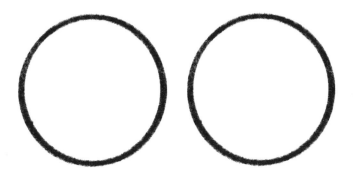

Paste your coins here.

Now draw what you think or want a coin to look like in the year you'll open this book again. Don't forget to write the year on your coin!

DATE: _____ 107

Here is a drawing of what I want to do when I grow up...

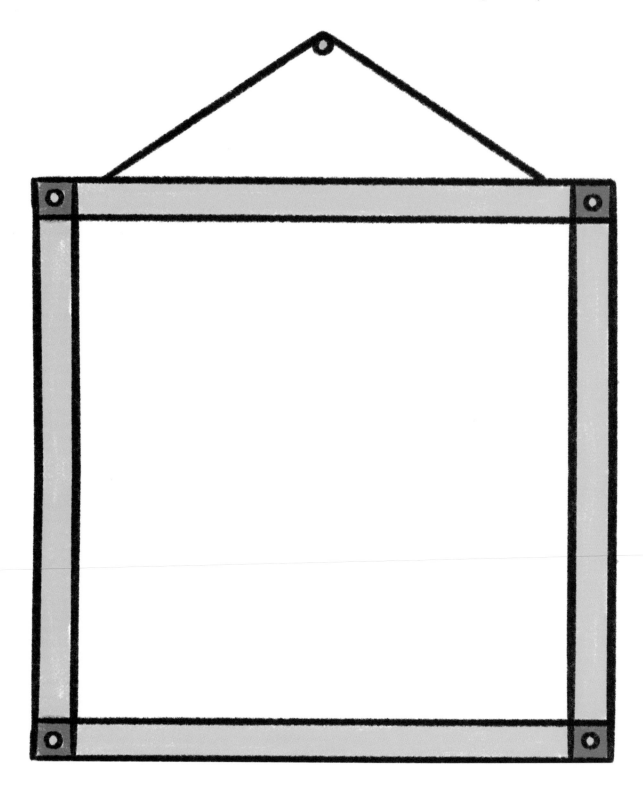

...and a portrait of what I might look like in the future.

Here are my future pets!

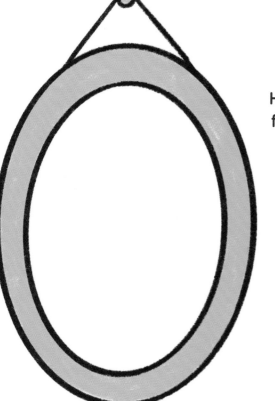

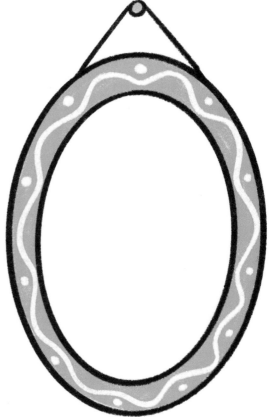

What do you think the world will be like when you are older and you read through this journal? Draw or write what you think will change and what might stay the same.

DATE: _____

Draw some gadgets you think might exist and what their functions will be.

MASH

Let's play MASH to predict your future! MASH stands for Mansion, Apartment, Shack, House. Here's how to play:

1. Write down your answers under each category.
2. Draw a spiral for five seconds in the bubble below. Count the number of rings in the spiral. That is your number!
3. Start with the Mansion at the top-left of the opposite page. Go clockwise, and count through your list of options. Stop when you get to your number. Cross out that option.
4. Continue counting options and crossing them off the page. Skip the ones you have already crossed off. When you get to the end of the list, go back to the top and keep counting and crossing off items.
5. Stop when you have one option in each category. Circle the options in each category that are left. That is your future!

DATE: _____

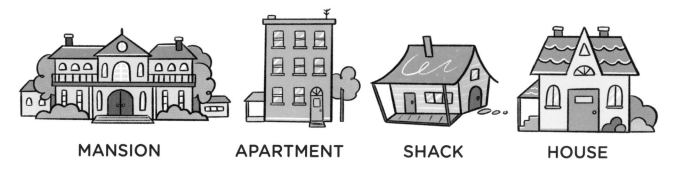

MANSION   APARTMENT   SHACK   HOUSE

LIFE PARTNER

_____
_____
_____
_____

NUMBER OF KIDS

_____
_____
_____
_____

JOB

_____
_____
_____
_____

CAR

_____
_____
_____
_____

PET

_____
_____
_____
_____

BEST FRIEND

_____
_____
_____
_____

MAKING A TIME CAPSULE

A time capsule is a collection of objects that are relevant to a point in time. What do you want your future-self to remember about your today-self? Here is how to make a time capsule to open when you are older.

STEP 1: PICK A TIME CAPSULE CONTAINER

Look around your house for a container to hold your treasures. If you pick a container that used to have food in it, make sure the container is clean and dry. Here are some good options:

- a pickle jar with a lid
- a canning jar with a lid
- an empty coffee can with a lid
- an unused paint can
- a plastic container with a lid

STEP 2: DECIDE WHAT TO ADD TO YOUR TIME CAPSULE

Fill your time capsule with things that are important to you!
Here are some suggestions:

- artwork and drawings
- photos of family and friends
- photos or mementos of memorable things you did this year
- notes from friends and family

- something with today's date
- a small toy
- schoolwork
- awards from school
- movie tickets
- coins

- receipts from your favorite store or restaurant
- stickers
- anything you want to remember!

Fill out the page on the right with the help of an adult. Color the reverse side of the page, and then cut the page out of the book. Roll up the page and tie it with a string or simply fold it up. Add it to your time capsule!

STEP 3: ADD THE DATE AND SEAL YOUR TIME CAPSULE

Cut out the label from page 121. Write today's date on it and paste the label on your time capsule. Cut out the tag that says when to open the time capsule and mark the date. Make sure you have included everything you want to save in your time capsule, and then close the lid.

STEP 4: LOOK FORWARD TO THE FUTURE

Put your time capsule in a safe place. Think of the fun you'll have when you open your time capsule years from now to check out each item!

ON THIS DAY

Today's date:_____

Temperature/weather today:_____

Home address: _____

Phone number:_____

Name of my school: _____

Where my parents work: _____

My country's leader:_____

My city's mayor: _____

My city's population: _____

News Headline 1: _____

News Headline 2: _____

News Headline 3: _____

A movie ticket costs: _____

A gallon of gas costs:_____

A postage stamp costs: _____

A gallon of milk costs: _____

Bestselling fiction book: _____

Bestselling non-fiction book: _____

No. 1 song: _____

Popular TV shows: _____

Popular YouTube channels: _____

Popular movies: _____

CUTOUTS

Use these cutouts to decorate this book and your time capsule.

Use these apples on page 64!

Punch a hole in this tag and
tie it to your time capsule.

DO NOT OPEN BEFORE

_____

Use the tag and one
of these labels on your
time capsule.

TIME
CAPSULE

time
Capsule

Add today's date
and your name to
the label.

Draw or paste a picture onto these frames, label them,
and include them in your time capsule!

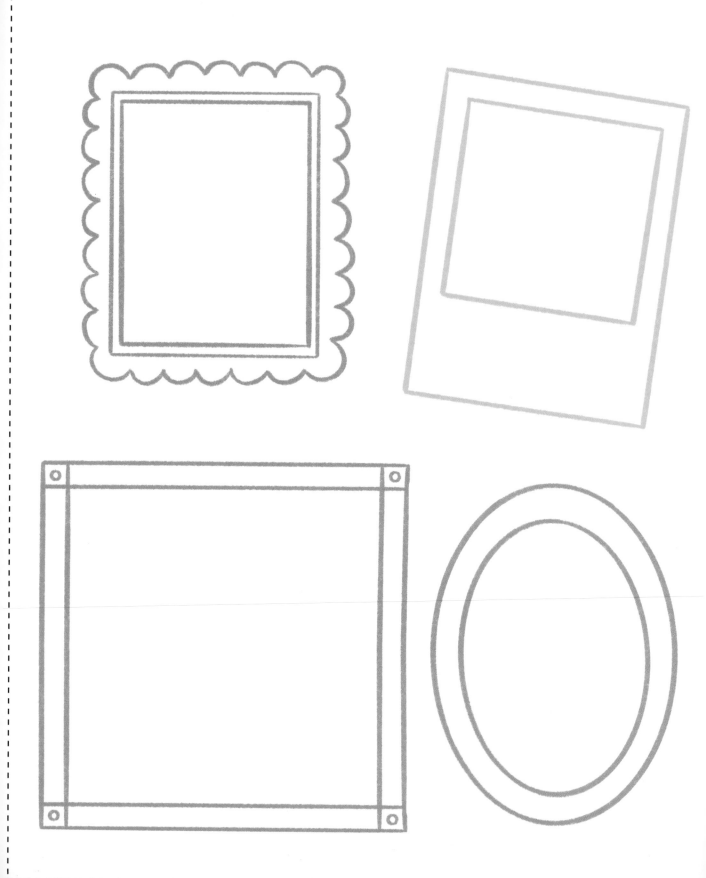

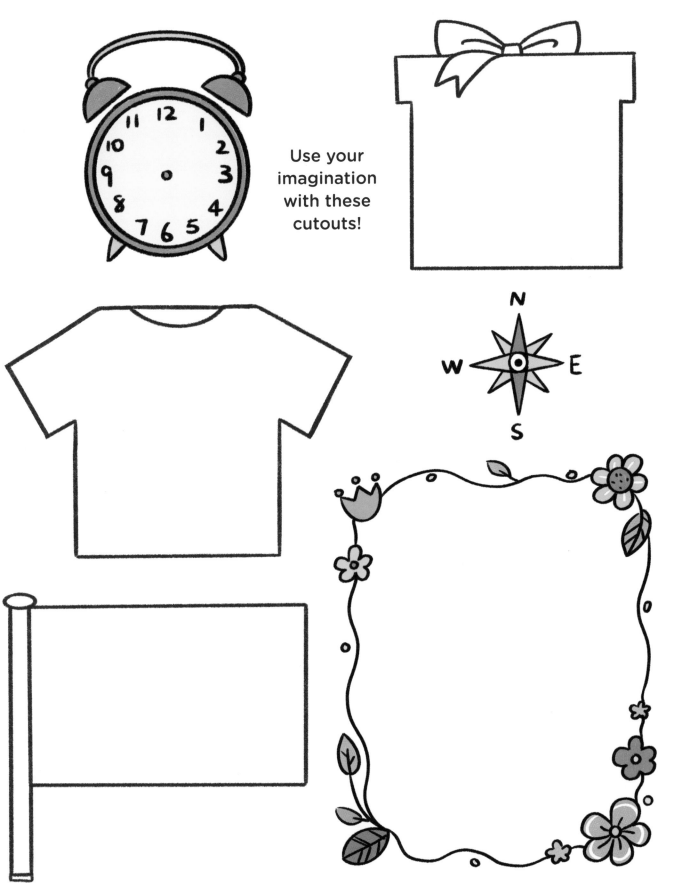

Use your imagination with these cutouts!

CONGRATULATIONS!

You've reached the end of your time capsule art journal. Once you decide when you want to open your journal again, write that date on a piece of tape. Use that tape to seal this journal so it can't easily be opened.

Before you seal your journal, make sure to go back to page 11 and write down the date you completed all the prompts and when you expect to open this book again.

Now it's time to seal the journal and put it in a safe place. Remember: Do not open your journal until the date you chose! Future You will thank you!

ABOUT THE ARTIST

Pamela (Xinyu) Chen is a young illustrator and designer from Xiamen, China. She earned a BFA Illustration degree from Columbus College of Art & Design (CCAD) in 2020 and has created illustrations for children's books, magazines, and product packaging. Pamela enjoys experimenting with different styles and techniques to achieve her ideal artwork. Much of her work is inspired by music, movies, fashion, books, and vintage toys.

Nicole Sipe is an editor for a Midwest parenting magazine and a children's book author. Born and raised in Southern California, Nicole traded the city and sun for corn and creeks, and now lives in Indiana with her husband, two sons, and Collie.